From Start to Finish

From Start to Finish

The Guide To Your Own Personal Credit Repair

Advanced Credit Solutions

This book was printed in the United States of America.

To order additional copies of this book, contact:
Xlibris Corporation
1-888-795-4274
www.Xlibris.com
Orders@Xlibris.com
38363

DISCLAIMER

While this report will help solve the average consumer's credit problems, it is with the understanding that the author/publisher is not an attorney and is not engaged in rendering legal advice. If legal assistance is required, the services of a competent professional should be sought.

The following information has been carefully researched and complied and is believed to be accurate at the time of publishing. However, neither the author nor publisher shall be held legally responsible for any loss or damages caused or alleged to have been caused directly or indirectly by such information.

CONTENTS

MISSION STATEMENT

OUR MISSION IS to bring awareness to the public on how important your credit score is and how everything you do affects it. We have developed this manual to make people self aware of their role and responsibility in maintaining good credit. More often than not people's credit scores are affected by their ability not to do it themselves. We are providing a service to assist the public, which will empower each individual to take control of their own credit history. All of the information provided in this manual has been researched and tested on real individuals over the past 8 years. With much success those who have used the information in this manual are debt free and in control of their credit. Once you receive this information you will be able to maintain your own credit information for life. This is our main goal for you to empower yourself. There are predatory organizations out there whose main goal is profit. Some companies will pull you in by stating their service is free when it is not. In fact, the service is never free and your credit is never repaired. This is where we come in. Using this manual will stop any organization from taking advantage of you. You can take matters in your own hands and fix your credit problems yourself. Our mission is to assist you in this process and to show you how easy it is to repair your credit. With patience, persistence and determination you to can be debt free and credit smart.

INTRODUCTION

THE INFORMATION IN this manual is up to date and accurate to the best of the author's knowledge. The author has had many years of credit repair experience, and has worked for a large credit repair agency. All of the guidelines of the Fair Credit Reporting Act are followed to assure your rights are protected when dealing with creditors and credit bureaus. These are the same guidelines credit repair agencies follow. We are providing this manual as a guide for the average consumer—anyone can repair their own credit as well or better than a credit repair agency.

In doing so, you can provide yourself with the best credit score possible. Your credit score has become the most important part of your financial future. Financial freedom has always been possible. Controlling your credit has never been easier. Advanced Credit Solutions soul purpose is to inform consumers' on how to maintain and repair their own credit. Just follow these simple guidelines and good credit will be your greatest reward.

CONSUMER GUIDE—
REPAIR YOUR CREDIT

ANY DEROGATORY ITEM *can be removed* from your credit report, including bankruptcies, judgments, liens, late pay etc.—*true or not*. According to the Fair Credit Reporting Act (F.C.R.A.) §611(a), if the information being disputed is found to be *inaccurate or can no longer be verified,* the Consumer Reporting Agency (credit bureau) shall promptly delete such information. The Bureau has to do this in a reasonable amount of time, 30 days constitutes this amount of time.

Remember all negative items can be removed. *This does not mean that they will be removed.* If, after reinvestigation, the disputed items on your report are found to be *true, accurate* and you have no proof of the contrary, you have three options:

1.   Continue sending your dispute letters, hoping your persistence will pay off;

2.   Negotiate a settlement with the creditor of an item that will not be otherwise removed; or

3.   Start with a brand new credit file.

There are millions of people nationwide with credit problems, due to various circumstances. Some may need the help of consolidating their bills. If you owe money on credit cards, medical bills, or student loans and you find it difficult to stay current, there is hope. There is a service, free to the consumer, which may be able to help you. They will negotiate a payment plan with your creditors on your behalf. Call Consumer Credit Counseling at (800) 215-9921. You will automatically be given the phone number of the office closest to your home and they will give you the full details of the program.

Although there is hundreds of small local credit reporting agencies, we are only concerned with the three major bureaus, EXPERIAN, TRANS-UNION, and EQUIFAX.

All credit bureaus large or small are dealt with in the exact same manner. The only reason you would bother with any of the smaller local bureaus is if you received a denial letter from a creditor listing that particular bureau as the one providing negative information on you. But, in all practicality, you will be dealing with the three national bureaus.

The first thing you need to do is request a copy of your credit report from each credit bureau. If married, you will need to get a copy of your spouse's report also. The reason for this is information has a tendency to merge from or to your spouse's file. This merging of information not only happens with married couples, but also family members, and people with similar names.

This information can also merge from one bureau file to another, because they sell information to one another, even though they are competitors.

All three bureaus will give you a free copy of your credit report if you have been denied credit within the past 60 days and that particular bureau was named in your denial letter from the creditor. Just send a copy of the denial letter along with your request for a free credit report.

Current listings for all three major credit bureaus are as follows:

EXPERIAN

POST OFFICE BOX 2104

ALLEN, TEXAS 75013-0949

(888) 397-3742 www.experian.com

The cost of the credit report varies from state to state and should be $8.00 or less. For more information call EXPERIAN directly at (800) 422-4879.

Trans-Union charges $8.00 for your credit report request if you do not qualify for a free report. Send your request to:

TRANS-UNION CORP.

POST OFFICE BOX 1000

Chester, PA 19022

(800) 888-4213 www.transunion.com

Equifax will provide customers with a credit report for $9.00 if they do not qualify for a free credit report. **NOTE: Residents of certain states may receive free reports. Contact Equifax directly for more information:**

EQUIFAX

POST OFFICE BOX 105851

ATLANTA, GA 30348

(800) 685-1111 www.equifax.com

Once you receive copies of your credit reports from all three bureaus, you should make two copies of each. Highlight all the negative entries on the photocopied reports and circle the items *that appear identically on each report.*

IMPORTANT: *Never* try to remove all negative entries at one time, especially with the denial method. The reason for this is, according to the F.C.R.A. §611(a), the consumer reporting agency (credit bureau) does not have grounds to investigate or delete negative information if "it has reasonable grounds to believe that the dispute by the consumer is frivolous or irrelevant." By denying all of the negative items at one time (as many credit repair companies attempt to accomplish), your requests seem frivolous. For greater success, try to pick out **two or three items** to dispute.

As mentioned earlier, the bureaus sell information to one another. Therefore, it is imperative to *dispute the identical negative items simultaneously* to avoid the risk of having the items on one bureaus file contaminating the file of other bureaus. Just send a copy of your credit report, with the two or three items you wish to contest circled in ink and staple it to the back of your dispute letter.

Remember, anything can be removed from your credit file, true or false, because the credit bureau must verify the accuracy of the information in a reasonable amount of time (30 days). As a general rule, **50%** of the negative items in your credit file will be removed with the dispute method. The best month to dispute the accuracy of your report is December. The holidays are a very busy time for creditors and credit bureaus and it is impossible to respond to a dispute in 30 days.

The easiest items to have removed from your credit file are those that do not belong there and you have proof of their inaccuracy. For example *obsolete information,* **bankruptcies (must be removed after ten years) liens, judgments, late pays, charge offs, repossessions (must be removed after seven years from the date of the last activity), bills that belong to your ex-spouse, late payments when you have the canceled check to**

proving timely payment, a loan you did not apply for, a negative item listed multiple times in a single report, etc.

But always remember, the burden of proof is on the creditor, and they must report back to the credit bureau in a timely manner. The creditor will, in many instances, fail to respond to the credit bureaus request for the verification of a disputed item. It may be that the creditor does not have the manpower to verify the information in a timely manner or they may no longer have the information on file. The reason is not important; the failure of the creditor to respond to the bureaus request will result in the removal of the disputed item.

Another problem is having unauthorized credit inquiries. This is most common when you go to a vehicle dealership and fill out a credit application. Let's say you went to three dealerships and each dealer sent your credit application out to four banks or finance companies for quick approval that means your credit report will reflect 12 different requests for credit. These inquires tend to give the impression that you are desperately going all over town to obtain a loan. In this instance, you must send a letter to the bureau(s) in question asking them to consolidate these inquires.

Bankruptcies, judgements and liens can be successfully removed through the denial process or challenging the different inaccuracies in the report including wrong names, dates, amounts, etc.

According to F.C.R.A. §602(b), consumers have the right to add positive supplementary credit history to their credit file. For example, you may have a loan on which you are paying off in good standing, car loan, or bank loan, which does not show up, on any of your credit reports.

You may have favorable information added to your credit file by sending the three bureaus a supplementary credit history request letter.

According to the F.C.R.A. §611(b), if the reinvestigation **does not resolve the dispute** you may file a brief statement of 100 words or less with the bureau explaining the reason for the negative entry. For example, you may have been laid off for several months, hospitalized or disabled (make sure that your statements are factual).

All correspondence to the credit bureaus should be sent by certified mail, return receipt requested. Keep accurate records—you should have three separate files, one for each bureau. Remember, if you do not receive a response from the bureau in 30 days; send another letter demanding a response according to your rights under F.C.R.A.

Once you have completed correcting your credit report, you will have the credit bureau send the latest (corrected) version of your report to anyone who has run a report on you for the last six months or employer(s) in the past two years, according to F.C.R.A. §611(d).

IMPORTANT NOTES:

The credit bureau may charge a small fee to add supplemental credit history to your file.

While challenging a tax lien if the government does not respond to the credit bureau in 30 days the bureau **must delete** *the tax lien notice and* **cannot reinstate it later.**

Tax files are generally transferred to archives after one year, thus increasing the time it takes to retrieve records making it next to impossible to make the 30-day deadline.

ADVANCED CREDIT SOLUTIONS

HOW TO GET AAA CREDIT IN 90 DAYS

THIS IS A very effective method for someone with little or no credit. If you have negative items on your credit report, they will need to be removed. This plan requires you to start with as little as $500.00, although you would be better off with $1,000.00. Borrow this from family or friends if necessary.

Let's assume you have $1,000.00 deposited in a savings account. After said funds have been in your account for at least 10 days, approach the loan officer about an insured loan against your deposited funds. Your bank will be happy to loan you money (in this case $1,000.00) against your savings, since they can always use the savings to pay off the loan if you were to default.

Take the $1,000.00 from the fourth bank and use it for the deposit for one or two secured credit cards. Once you receive your credit card, go to two or three major department stores that offer **instant credit** and use your MasterCard or VISA to qualify for said instant credit. If they check your credit, they will see that you have four open bank loans and you will be approved. To have an active credit account in these stores, you must put them to use. Use these cards to purchase items within reason. The object is not to overspend. **Your MasterCard or VISA may be used for anything**

including groceries, this happens to be an excellent way to use your credit card without getting yourself into needless debt. After you have made timely payments for a few months on your bank loans and credit cars, you will have an AAA credit rating.

WHAT YOU NEED TO KNOW ABOUT THE FAIR CREDIT REPORTING ACT

Fair Credit Reporting Act (F.C.R.A.) §611. Procedure in case of disputed accuracy

"(a) If the completeness or accuracy of any item of information contained in his file is disputed by a consumer, and such dispute is directly conveyed to the consumer reporting agency by the consumer, the consumer reporting agency shall within a reasonable amount of time reinvestigate and record the current status for that information unless it has reasonable grounds to believe that the dispute is frivolous and irrelevant. If after such reinvestigation such information is found to be inaccurate or can no longer be verified, the consumer reporting agency shall promptly delete such information. The presence of contradictory information in the consumer's file does not constitute reasonable grounds for believing the dispute is frivolous or irrelevant."

"(b)   If the reinvestigation does not resolve the dispute, the consumer may file a brief statement setting forth the nature of the dispute. The consumer-reporting agency may limit the statements to not more than one hundred words if it provides the consumer with assistance writing a clear summary of the dispute.

"(c)   Whenever a statement of a dispute is filed, unless there are reasonable grounds to believe it is frivolous and irrelevant, the consumer reporting agency shall, in any subsequent consumer report containing the information question, clearly note that is disputed by the consumer and provide either the consumers statement or a clear and accurate codification or summary thereof.

"(d)   Following any deletion of information which is found to be inaccurate or whose accuracy can no longer be verified or any notation as to disputed information, the consumer reporting agency shall, at the request of the consumer, furnish notification that the item has been deleted or the statement, codification or summary pursuant to subsection (b) or (c) to any person specifically designated by the consumer who has within two years prior thereto received a consumer report for employment purposes, or within the last six months prior thereto received a consumer report for any other purpose, which contained the deleted or disputed information. The consumer-reporting agency shall clearly and conspicuously disclose to the consumer his rights to make such a request. Such disclosure shall be made prior to the time the information is deleted or the customer's statement regarding disputed information is received.

§612. Charges for certain disclosures.

". . . no charge may be made for notifying such persons of the deletion of information which is found to be inaccurate or which can no longer be verified."

§619. Obtaining information under false pretenses.

"Any person who knowingly and willfully obtains information on a consumer from a consumer reporting agency under false pretences shall be fined not more than $5,000 of imprisoned not more than one year, or both."

UNDERSTANDING YOUR CREDIT SCORE

IN REPAIRING YOUR credit you need to understand your **Credit Score**. Of course, we know the higher your credit score the chances are better for you to purchase a home, a car, a business, etc. Furthermore, what a large amount of us don't realize is you cannot get your actual credit score without requesting it. If you request your credit reports without indicating you want your credit score you will receive your credit reports without the scores.

Besides the information on the credit report the score is one of the most vital parts of your report. In knowing your credit score it will give you an idea of where you fall in the excellent to poor spectrum.

Here are the actual Credit Score ranges:

750-850   Excellent

660-749   Good

620-659   Fair

350-619   Poor

Understanding this about your credit score makes it easy for you to navigate through your credit reports.

IDENTITY THEFT

*I*DENTITY THEFT HAS become a big problem over the recent years. Crooks use many means to obtain your personal information from going through your trash, to hacking into company computers, to phone scams and many other methods. One suggestion in preventing this from happening to you is always be careful when discarding personal information like your social security number and birth date. Crooks can use this information to rob you blind. Also, when using your computers protect your identity by using secure websites that will not give out your personal information to unauthorized persons. Also, use the security lock features most computers have now to block anyone from accessing your personal information. It's a good idea to check all three-credit reports each month to make sure there is no unauthorized activity.

If you do become a victim of identity theft, you should contact the credit bureaus immediately. The credit bureaus can put a fraud alert on your reports at no charge to you. (*Note: You must call or write all three credit bureaus to activate this. It's also a good idea to do this even if your identity is not stolen.*) Contact any and all credit card companies, banking institutions and any other agencies you have credit with. Keep a record of everyone you spoke to regarding this situation. It can take anywhere from 3 months to years to fix your identity profile. So, please take every precaution to protect your identity.

FREEZING YOUR CREDIT

ANOTHER METHOD OF protecting your credit after identity theft is freezing your credit entirely. *Credit Freezing* is something fairly new as a method of protecting yourself against identity theft. It allows you the victim of identity theft to have your credit reports locked from prying eyes. No one will have access to any of your credit information and it will prevent any possible fraudulent activity to occur again. Once again you will have to contact all three credit bureaus to have the process done. The service is free if you're an identity theft victim otherwise the fee is $10 per bureau. Each bureau will give you a personal identification number to be used in the event you want to unlock your credit history. If you as a consumer want to unlock or "thaw" your credit you will have to pay an additional fee to do so. It will take about 3 days for the bureaus to lift the freeze.

Know that those of identity theft are not the only ones able to use this method. Consumers who have established enough credit or if you just are worried about becoming a victim of identity theft can also use this method to protect themselves. As the consumer you have the right to protect you credit.

There are a number of states who have passed credit protection laws to be able to freeze credit reports. Some states have limits on freezing only reserved for identity theft victims. Check to make sure your state isn't one of them. For more information on protecting your identity go to your states local governmental website.

DISPUTE LETTERS—EXAMPLES

THESE LETTERS WERE created to assist you the consumer on how to write a dispute letter. Credit agencies or collection bureaus, vendors, etc. require a dispute letter to verify your request. Please feel free to use the proper template letter for your own needs. These letters make it easier for you to track the process of your credit repair process.

Letter #1   Request for Credit Report

Letter #2   Dispute or denial letter

Letter #3   Items that belong to a former spouse

Letter #4   Merging of inquiries

Letter #5   Reminder to respond to any of the above three letters

Letter #6   Demand for corrected report if Letter #4 fails to get a response within 30 days

Letter #7   "Consumer Statement"

Letter #8   Supplemental credit history

Letter #9   Letter to a company that illegally ran a credit report on you

LETTER #1

Date

Name of Credit Bureau

Street Address

City, State, Zip

Attn: Customer Relations Dept.

Dear Sir/Madame:

Please send me a copy of my credit report. The information needed is provided below.

Full name (include Jr., Sr., I, II, III)

Name of Spouse

Present Address, City State, Zip

Previous Address for past 5 years if different from above

Date of Birth

Social Security Number

Please find attached a copy of my current utility bill or a copy of my driver's license.

Yes my credit has been denied within the last 60 days, a copy of the denial letter is attached. Please send my report free of charge. No, my credit has not been denied within the last 60 days. Please find a check enclosed in the amount of $ _____.

Thank you in advance for your prompt response to my request.

Sincerely,

Your signature

LETTER #2

Full Name

Street Address

City, State, Zip

Date of Birth

Social Security Number

Date

Name of Credit Bureau

Address

City, State, Zip

Attn: Customer Relations Dept.

Dear Sir/Madame:

After reviewing my credit report, I noticed the following inaccuracies. I have marked the items in ink on the attached copy of my report.

Please investigate and delete these items as required by the Fair Reporting Act §611(a). It should be understood that failure to re-verify within 30 days constitutes non-verification and these items must be deleted promptly.

As provided by the Fair Credit Reporting Act §611(d) and §612, please send me a free copy of my updated and corrected credit report as notification that the inaccurate information has been deleted.

Sincerely,

Your signature

LETTER #3

Full Name

Street Address

City, State, Zip

Date of Birth

Social Security Number

Date

Name of Credit Bureau

Address

City, State, Zip

Attn: Customer Relations Dept.

Dear Sir/Madame:

After reviewing my credit report, I noticed the following items that do not belong on my report. They belong to my former spouse. These inaccuracies are marked in pen on the attached report.

Please reinvestigate and delete these disputed items, to reflect my true credit history as required by the Fair Reporting Act §611(a). It should be understood that failure to re-verify within 30 days constitutes non-verification and these items must be deleted promptly.

As provided by the Fair Credit Reporting Act §611(d) and §612, please send me a free copy of my updated and corrected credit report as notification that the inaccurate information has been deleted.

Sincerely,

Your signature

LETTER #4

Full Name

Street Address

City, State, Zip

Date of Birth

Social Security Number

Date

Name of Credit Bureau

Address

City, State, Zip

Attn: Customer Relations Dept.

Dear Sir/Madame:

After reviewing my credit report I located the following problems of inaccurate reporting. I have marked the items in pen on the attached report.

The presence of the inquiries as entries separate from the resulting accounts inaccurately duplicates information. The inquiry entry should be removed or at least merged into the accounts to which they belong.

Please reinvestigate and delete these disputed items, to reflect my true credit history as required by the Fair Reporting Act §611(a). It should be understood that failure to re-verify within 30 days constitutes non-verification and these items must be deleted promptly.

As provided by the Fair Credit Reporting Act §611(d) and §612, please send me a free copy of my updated and corrected credit report as notification that the inaccurate information has been deleted.

Sincerely,

Your signature

LETTER #5

Full Name

Street Address

City, State, Zip

Date of Birth

Social Security Number

Date

Name of Credit Bureau

Address

City, State, Zip

Attn: Customer Relations Dept.

Dear Sir/Madame:

Thirty days ago your firm received a letter disputing inaccurate and incomplete items listed on my credit report issued by your company.

Please note that 30 days is considered a "reasonable time" under the Fair Credit Reporting Act §611(a) for a re-verification of the erroneous items.

I have not received a reply from you within 30 days, therefore, the information on my credit report was either inaccurate or it could not be verified. According to the Fair Credit Reporting Act §611(a), the items must be deleted immediately.

As provided by the Fair Credit Reporting Act §611(d) and §612, please send me a free copy of my updated and corrected credit report as notification that the inaccurate information has been deleted.

Sincerely,

Your signature

LETTER #6

Full Name

Street Address

City, State, Zip

Date of Birth

Social Security Number

Date

Name of Credit Bureau

Address

City, State, Zip

Attn: Customer Relations Dept.

Dear Sir/Madame:

On *date of last letter* I wrote a letter to your company asking that you verify the items I had identified as inaccurate or incomplete on my credit report. I have attached copies of both letters for your review.

I assume that you have not been able to verify the information I have disputed. You must, therefore, comply with the provision of the Fair Credit Reporting Act §611(a) and delete the disputed items from my report.

As provided by the Fair Credit Reporting Act §611(d) and §612, please send me a free copy of my updated and corrected credit report as notification that the inaccurate information has been deleted.

If I do not receive an updated copy of my credit report, with the disputed items removed, I will have no choice but to seek legal remedy as provided under the Fair Credit Reporting Act §616 "civil liability for willful noncompliance". Your bureau may be liable for damages both actual and punitive as well as court costs, including attorney's fees.

A copy of this letter has been forwarded to the Federal Trade Commission.

Sincerely,

Your signature

LETTER #7

Full Name

Street Address

City, State, Zip

Date of Birth

Social Security Number

Date

Name of Credit Bureau

Address

City, State, Zip

Attn: Customer Relations Dept.

Dear Sir/Madame:

Since reinvestigation has not resolved my dispute, I want the following statement included in my report, as provided by the Fair Credit Reporting Act §611(b). I understand that the "consumer statement" must be no more than 100 words. I assume that 30 days is a reasonable time for the completing of this update.

Use this space for your consumer statement or attach your statement to this letter.

According to the Fair Credit Reporting Act §611(b) and §612, please send me a free copy of my updated credit report, with the above statement included.

Sincerely,

Your signature

LETTER #8

Full Name

Street Address

City, State, Zip

Date of Birth

Social Security Number

Date

Name of Credit Bureau

Address

City, State, Zip

Attn: Customer Relations Dept.

Dear Sir/Madame:

According to the Fair Credit Reporting Act (FCRA), Section 602(b) "It is the purpose of the title (FCRA) to require that the consumer reporting agencies adopt reasonable procedures for the meeting of the needs of commerce for consumer credit, personnel, insurance, and other information in a manner which is fair and equitable for the consumer, with regard to the confidentiality, accuracy, relevancy, and proper utilization of such information in accordance with the requirements of this title." The intent of the FCRA included recording supplementary credit information if requested by a consumer.

I hereby request that you add the attached history of payments.

Please inform me within 30 days of your compliance with the section §611 requirements that a consumer's credit report should reflect 'completeness and accuracy" within a "reasonable" time after notification by the consumer.

Sincerely,

Your signature

LETTER #9

Full Name

Street Address

City, State, Zip

Date of Birth

Social Security Number

Date

Name of Credit Bureau

Address

City, State, Zip

Attn: Customer Relations Dept.

Dear Sir/Madame:

After reviewing my credit report, it has come to my attention that your company on *date of inquiry* illegally ran a credit report on me. At no time had I given you authorization to do this. Your company has violated my rights under the Fair Credit Reporting Act §619 and this inquiry is injurious to my credit rating.

Unless you immediately contact the credit bureau and remedy this situation, I will take legal action. According to the F.C.R.A. §619, you are liable for a $5000.00 fine or up to one year in prison or both.

Sincerely,

Your signature

www.ingramcontent.com/pod-product-compliance
Lightning Source LLC
Chambersburg PA
CBHW061223280526
45784CB00006B/2606